Sarah —
    To the
best of fortune —
The Vieux Carre.

            Fred
                2/13/90

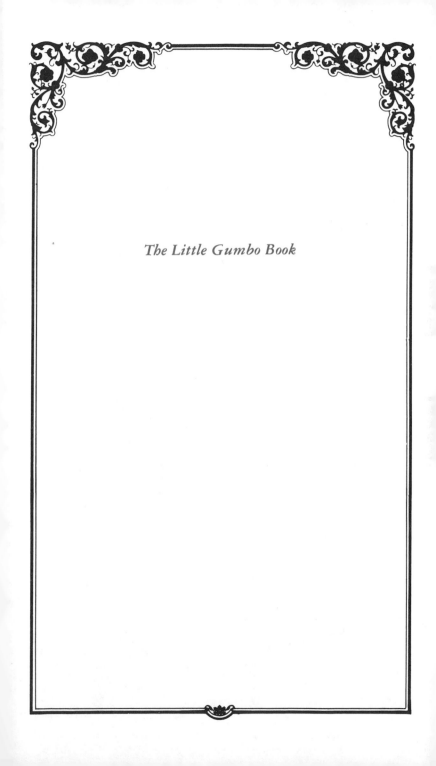

The Little Gumbo Book

Acadian Village and Tropical Gardens. Lafayette.

The Little GUMBO Book

◆

*TWENTY-SEVEN
CAREFULLY CREATED
RECIPES
THAT WILL ENABLE
EVERYONE
TO ENJOY
THE
SPECIAL
EXPERIENCE
OF
GUMBO*

by
Gwen McKee

Illustrations by Tupper Davidson

QUAIL RIDGE PRESS
Baton Rouge/Brandon

DEDICATION

To my husband, Barney,
who suggested *The Little Gumbo Book*
several years ago,
and who persisted till it became a reality.

CONTENTS

PREFACE

Ahhhhh . . . *gumbo*. The word itself conjures up warmth and contentment sitting before a steamy bowl of this healthy, rich, Creole dish. Ummmmm . . . *gumbo*. The thought of it sends that delightfully tantalizing aroma to your senses—and you to the market for the ingredients!

The word *gumbo* comes from the African *kingumbo* which means *okra*. And *okra*, a long, fuzzy green vegetable pod which came from Africa, is one of gumbo's characteristic ingredients. Besides being a tasty vegetable, it is a thickener. Then came *filé* (FEE lay) which can be traced back to the South Louisiana Choctaw Indians who made a kind of powder from ground sassafras leaves and brought it to the French Market in New Orleans to be sold for medicinal purposes. The Creoles liked the delicate flavor and began using it in their soups and stews. They found that besides adding flavor, filé also thickened with the same slippery smoothness of okra, and could be substituted when okra wasn't in season. Creole cooks began many of their dishes with a *roux* (ROO)—the slow browning of flour. They discovered roux gave additional thickening and flavoring to their gumbo. The remaining ingredients consisted of pieces of seafood or fowl or game or meat with their cooking liquid and an assortment of creole seasonings. And then it was served over rice. Today the same secret of that fine Creole cooking holds true—it lies in the artful blending of all these unique flavors in one glorious gumbo pot!

I have a passion for gumbo. I have served gumbo at more dinner parties than any other dish, if not as the entrée, in a cup before the main meal. No guest has ever failed to compliment it—and they usually ask for seconds! It can be a lot of fun to prepare, it can be very inexpensive (even with costly seafood ingredients, the price per bowl is still a bargain), it can be made with low-cal ingredients, and it is quite nourishing. And the best reason of all to make gumbo is that it is so delicious!

The recipes in this book have been compiled over a number of years from a variety of sources. As a collector of cookbooks and editor of all Quail Ridge Press cookbooks (including *Best of the Best from Louisiana*), I have had the pleasure of testing many gumbo recipes which originated in humble bayou kitchens, renowned South Louisiana restaurants, and the kitchens of people who enjoy creating memorable meals. With the help of many of my good friends, several of whom had never made gumbo before, the task of testing, adjusting, adding, deleting and sampling was generally more fun than work. I am particularly grateful to Barbara Moseley, Waynell Harris, Jean Harrison, Doris Bradshaw, Dan Taylor, Virginia Pennington, and Mary Tucker for their gumbo testing, opinions, and editing, and to Carol Mead for her word editing. Bruce Morgan at the Louisiana Office of Tourism is always so friendly and helpful. And you can look at Al Godoy's lovely photographs and almost smell the gumbo simmering on a stove not very far away.

Gumbo is considered to be the national dish of Louisiana. Few who visit the state fail to enjoy it; they wish they could recreate this delectable dish at home. It is my hope that this book will eliminate the fears of those who have been afraid to tackle making gumbo. For them I've included the *Step-by-Step to Great Gumbo*—a walk-through recipe with lots of whats and whys and hows, suggestions for substitutions, and explanations all along the way. Also, there is *All About Roux*, with six different ways to make it, and *A Word About Rice*, with various cooking methods suggested. And further, there is a recipe for *K's Cajun Seasoning*, which offers a make-it-yourself solution for those who are not able to buy packaged Creole seasoning. And there are reminders throughout the book—for which I beg the reader's for-giveness—that gumbo is even better the next day or after freezing. It bears repeating.

My research has taught me much about the old and new methods used in making gumbo, including iron pot, crock pot, and microwave. I have also learned that everybody has his/her own unique way of making this very special dish that no other recipe can rival. I hope that after trying some of these recipes, you will be motivated to create your very own special gumbo recipe, too. My friend, the show is yours!

Gwen McKee

THE WOOD STOVE
WAS THE HEART OF
THE KITCHEN FOR
GENERATIONS...
IT GOBBLED CORDS
OF WOOD, BLACKEN-
ING POTS OF THE
FRENCH CUISINE
WHERE ROUX,
ETOUFFÉE AND
SAUCE PIQUANT
ORIGINATED.

Loreauville Heritage Museum. Near New Iberia.

ALL ABOUT ROUX

No self-respecting Cajun would dream of making gumbo without a roux. The browning of the flour takes away the raw pasty taste of white flour and gives it a nut-like, roasted flavor that is so wonderfully Creole. Roux also adds a degree of thickness and richness that sets gumbo a world apart from ordinary soup.

A roux is simply a mixture of flour and fat cooked and stirred till it is brown. Slowly heating the flour breaks up the starch molecules and reduces its thickening power while giving it a unique, scorchy flavor at the same time. The degree of doneness is determined by the color, which gets darker the longer it is cooked. Every imaginable brown color comparison has been used to describe roux (mahogany, coffee, pecan).

Roux is also made with shortening and many kinds of cooking oil, including olive oil. Or even mixtures of oil and butter, bacon drippings and oil, or any combination. Any of these mixed with flour will make a dark roux (walnut, chocolate, dark caramel).

A mixture of flour and butter is a French roux. This is cooked more slowly until it is bubbly, but not browned. Colors used to describe this light roux are peanut butter, café au lait (coffee with milk), copper penny, and light caramel.

Now about proportions—equal amounts of flour and oil are the most common measurements for those who measure. Once you become a "roux maker," you will probably do it by feel. When forced to measure, I found I was a little heavier on flour. But there are those who insist a little more oil is best. The end result should be the consistency of thin pudding.

In most recipes, the chopped vegetables are added to the roux as soon as it reaches the desired color. Their addition will darken the color very slightly, then arrest the cooking temperature and prevent the roux from scorching. The vegetables will get soft in a short amount of time. In some recipes, hot water is then added (cold water may make the mixture curdle) to make it smooth and easy to mix in with the other ingredients. But do add vegetables or water, or remove the roux from the skillet, as it will continue to brown even with the heat off.

The only thing that can go wrong with roux is that you can let it burn. The secret is very simple—keep stirring till it's brown! And don't go for a very dark roux on your first try. The next color beyond charcoal brown is burned black. Once you get the hang of it, it is really quite simple and actually fun to make. We Louisianians think a dark, smooth, rich roux is absolutely *beautiful!* It is the perfect overture to the masterpiece we are about to create!

BAKED ROUX

3 cups flour
3 cups vegetable oil

Mix flour and oil in iron skillet or heavy oven-proof container. Bake in preheated 400-degree oven 1½–2 hours, stirring every 15 minutes. The color determines the doneness (coffee with cream, caramel, pecan, milk chocolate—you know, that rich "roux" color). Cool before storing. May be frozen.

NOTE: This recipe can be increased or decreased—just use equal amounts of flour and oil.

IRON SKILLET ROUX
Gwen's favorite—I like to stir!

¾ cup vegetable oil
1 cup flour

Stir together over medium high heat in a big iron skillet till medium brown. Add whatever chopped vegetables you plan to use and keep stirring till the vegetables are soft—adding the vegetables arrests the cooking temperature and will prevent the roux from scorching. I add ½ cup hot water gradually while stirring until smooth. Ready to add to the rest of your masterpiece!

SKILLET DRY ROUX

Place 1–2 cups of flour in an iron skillet on medium heat and stir constantly with a wooden spoon till the flour is the color of the outside of pecans (takes about 15 minutes). Cool and store in a jar. To use: Mix equal parts of dry roux and water or oil, stirring till smooth.

OVEN-BAKED DRY ROUX
This is made with no oil!

Simply distribute 2–6 cups of flour evenly over the dry bottom of a big iron skillet or heavy Dutch oven and put it in a 400-degree oven for about an hour. Stir it about every 15 minutes or so to brown evenly. Let cool and store in a jar.

TO USE: Simply mix equal parts dry roux and water till smooth. Add to gumbo, soups, gravies for thickening. Perfect! And you haven't used any grease at all!

You may also add an equal portion of dry roux to heated oil in a skillet (no need to brown).

MICROWAVE ROUX (WITH VEGETABLES)
Grandmother would even be fooled by this one!

2/3 cup vegetable oil
2/3 cup flour
2/3 cup chopped onions
2/3 cup chopped celery
2/3 teaspoon minced garlic
2/3 cup chopped bell pepper
2/3 cup chopped green onions (optional)
2/3 cup hot water

Mix oil with flour in a 4-cup glass measuring bowl. Microwave uncovered on HIGH for 6 minutes. Stir and cook another 30–60 seconds on HIGH till the color of mahogany.

Now you can add your chopped vegetables, stir well, and "sauté" them on HIGH for another 5 minutes till soft but not brown.

Now before stirring, pour oil off top. Add hot tap water, stirring till smooth. Beautiful! And it freezes for later use.

NOTE: This recipe can be increased to 1 of everything

(rather than ⅔), but put it in an 8-quart measure and increase the cooking times about 30 seconds each time. Or use ½. I just love this recipe—it's so easy to remember how much of everything to use! Oh, and frozen chopped vegetables work just fine—they just sizzle a bit more and require a few more seconds cooking time.

CREOLE ROUX

3 slices bacon
3 ounces smoked ham, diced (optional)
3 tablespoons flour
6 medium onions, finely chopped
3 stalks celery, finely chopped
1 bell pepper, finely chopped
3 pods garlic, minced
1 cup hot water
1 lemon (juice and pulp)
1 tablespoon Worcestershire
1 tablespoon Tabasco
1 tablespoon *K's Cajun Seasoning,*
(or salt and pepper)
1 teaspoon thyme
2 bay leaves

Fry bacon in heavy Dutch oven. Remove bacon and fry ham; remove ham. Add flour and stir constantly to make brown roux. Add vegetables and stir till soft. Add hot water, lemon juice and pulp and seasonings. Allow to simmer 30 minutes. Remove bay leaves. If desired, add bacon and ham scraps back to pot.

NOTE: This can be doubled and it freezes well!

Louisiana . . . a sportsman's paradise.

A WORD ABOUT RICE

A gumbo just wouldn't be a gumbo without rice! Occasionally rice is cooked in the gumbo pot, but most often it is cooked separately and the gumbo is served over it. Though it is not necessary, some people like to wash rice before it is cooked. Most any white rice is fine whether it is long or short grain (most prefer long grain), or converted or quick-cooking or boil-in-a-bag. Though package directions will tell you how to cook it, here are a few popular ways to prepare rice.

Steam it. Put 2 cups hot water, 1 teaspoon salt, and 1 cup rice in a 2- or 3-quart pot with a good-fitting lid. Bring to a boil, stir, turn down to simmer, cover, and cook about 20 minutes, or until water is absorbed. (Or if you're lucky enough to have a rice cooker, you get perfectly steamed rice every time!) This will make enough rice for 5–6 bowls of gumbo.

Boil it. Put any amount (up to 4 cups) of rice in a lot (about 3 quarts) of boiling, salted water in a big pot. Boil (uncovered) for about 15 minutes—do not overcook as it will get gummy. Best way to tell is to taste it. If there is no hard center, it's done! Drain rice in a colander and rinse with hot water. To keep it hot, place the colander over a pot of simmering water and put a pot lid over the rice. Some like to "sweat" boiled rice in a low oven for 10–20 minutes.

Bake it. Put 3 cups rice, 4 cups water, and 1½ teaspoons salt in a 9 × 13-inch baking pan. A little vinegar will make the rice more white; a little butter, more flavorful. Cover very tightly with foil and bake for about 45 minutes at 350 degrees (or use 2 cups converted rice, 3 cups water, and 1 teaspoon salt). With the help of a time-bake oven, the baking method cooks the rice while you're away.

Microwave it. Boil 2 cups lightly salted water in a 2-quart bowl or casserole. Add 1 cup rice, cover with waxed paper, and cook on HIGH 5 minutes. Stir, re-cover, and cook another 5–7 minutes on HIGH. Let it stand a few minutes before serving. This will be enough for 6–8 bowls of gumbo.

The usual serving amount is ½–⅔ cup cooked rice per bowl of gumbo. One cup of raw rice equals 3½ cups cooked rice.

And furthermore . . . rice freezes beautifully so don't be afraid to cook large amounts. Freeze flat in Zip-Loc bags (so you can break off as much as you need), or in small containers. To ready for serving, put the frozen rice in a colander and run hot water over it. Or microwave it right in the bag, opened slightly, for about a minute on HIGH. Don't put frozen rice in gumbo without thawing it first—it really needs to be brought back to life on its own!

K'S CAJUN SEASONING
*Once you start using it,
you'll never be without it!*

1 (26-ounce) box salt (or Lite Salt)
3 tablespoons black pepper
2 tablespoons garlic powder
1 teaspoon onion powder
1 teaspoon nutmeg
2 tablespoons Accent (optional)
2 tablespoons dried parsley flakes
4 tablespoons red pepper (Cayenne)
2 tablespoons chili powder

Mix all in large bowl or coffee can. Fill a shaker for daily use; store remainder in tightly covered container.

NOTE: This is quick to fix and is such a marvelous blend of seasonings that it enhances all it touches. It is not as peppery as most packaged creole seasonings and therefore lets the *seasoning* taste come through. Created by my good friends Kay and Francis Fuselier from Eunice, Louisiana, the fame of this wonderful seasoning is spreading. And you can't buy it—you have to make it or be fortunate enough to have a good friend make up a batch and share it with you! Poured in large, dial-type shakers with a bow tied around, "K's" makes a delightful "happy" at gift-giving time—they'll think of you every time they use it! (And, believe me, that will be often!)

An archway of Louisiana oak trees adorned with graceful Spanish moss.

STEP-BY-STEP TO GREAT GUMBO
A how-to recipe with lots of leeway
for creativity

PREPARATION:

The first thing you will need is a very big pot (a stock pot, canner, or spaghetti cooker is ideal because you want lots of room to add and stir; a Dutch oven will do for recipes serving fewer than 8 bowls), a heavy skillet for the roux (black iron is best), a pot to cook the rice in, measuring spoons and cups, a sharp knife, and a big spoon (I like wooden, but any long-handled spoon will do). And though it is certainly not essential, I recommend one more thing: an extra day—gumbo is so much better made ahead. Now read the recipe through to be sure you have all the ingredients. Procedure is important, so follow the steps as they come.

VEGETABLES:
3 cups chopped vegetables
(onions, green onions, celery, bell pepper)
½ teaspoon minced garlic,
(or 1 teaspoon garlic powder)
10 ounces cut okra

Get the vegetables chopped and ready first. (Cajuns often refer to onions, celery and bell pepper as "The Holy Trinity.") You can use either fresh or frozen chopped onion, green onion, and bell pepper, and either fresh minced garlic or garlic powder or granules (not garlic salt—it is merely salt with garlic flavor). Use what you like best (or have on hand). I recommend 1½ cups onions, and ½ cup each celery, green onion, and bell pepper, but any combination is fine. Put all these chopped vegetables together in one bowl.

If using fresh okra, wipe each pod with a clean cloth to remove fuzz, then slice thinly and have ready in a bowl. If using a box of frozen okra, remove the paper, open the package and have it ready, separated from the other chopped vegetables.

ROUX:

½ cup vegetable oil
½ cup flour

All it takes to make roux is the ability to stir and a bit of patience. It's fine to substitute shortening, bacon drippings, olive oil, lard or butter for any kind of vegetable oil. Of course the taste will vary a bit, but being creative is what gumbo is all about! An iron skillet or iron Dutch oven offers the most even heating, but any heavy skillet or pot will do.

Heat the oil on medium high heat about 2 minutes, then sprinkle on flour. I have a long wooden spoon with a flat end that works well, but any big spoon or whisk will do. Now this is going to take about 12–15 minutes of constant stirring. Amuse yourself by watching the colors change and trying to identify the color by a comparison. It will change from cream to beige to caramel to reddish-brown. The smell will begin to form at the beige stage. (Don't be discouraged by cries of "What's burning?" from those who have never had the pleasure of smelling roux before.) There are those who think roux is too hard to make because of the risk of burning it. The only way you can burn it is if you stop stirring it, or if you cook it too long. (If it turns black or has bits of charred pieces in it, it's time to throw it out and start over.) You will know when it is ready by the lovely scorchy smell, the nice thin-pudding texture, and the rich mahogany brown color.

Now add the chopped vegetables all at once to the

roux while continuing to stir. You will note that the color darkens slightly from a red brown to a real chocolate brown. The vegetables will arrest the cooking, so the roux will get no darker. After stirring for about 2 minutes, add the okra, lower the heat to medium, and stir for another 2 minutes. Now look what's happening! It becomes stringy and thickens as the okra cooks down. (Okra can be added at other times as you will note in different recipes, but this is probably easiest.) You can take a break now and stir occasionally for about 15 minutes, after which time it will look like several melted Nestle's Crunch bars—which is to say it is now smooth and thick and holding together nicely.

Stir roux, chopped tomatoes, and seasonings into stock (discussed in detail below). Heat till near boiling, lower heat and simmer, uncovered, one hour, then add main ingredients. At this point you will have repeated to yourself a dozen times, "Is this really worth it?" Have heart. And patience. This is a gourmet dish—it takes time, and is most definitely worth every minute of it.

TOMATOES:
1 pound, chopped

Some people make gumbo without tomatoes, so it's perfectly okay to simply skip this step. But most gumbo recipes call for some form of tomatoes. Fresh or canned tomatoes can be used, or canned stewed tomatoes, or Rotel tomatoes (leave out the red pepper in the recipe). Some substitute tomato juice, tomato sauce, or tomato paste. The paste is very dominant and will give the gumbo a strong tomatoey taste, so use it sparingly—½ of a 6-ounce can is plenty to substitute for the tomatoes in this recipe. Be sure to chop canned whole tomatoes as well as fresh. It seems the soft canned tomatoes would fall apart by themselves, and most will, but do encourage them a bit by pouring the can in a soup bowl and cutting through the tomatoes a few times with a knife. Or put the tomatoes in a blender or food processor for a few whirls.

STOCK:
5 cups stock

Of all the ingredients, I would have to say that the stock is *the* secret ingredient for making gumbo rich and flavorful. The stock is the broth or juice from cooking whatever it is you plan to make gumbo with.

Chicken stock is made by boiling the chicken parts till tender in seasoned water. Place the cleaned chicken in a stock pot, cover completely with water (about 2½ quarts), bring to a boil, and simmer, covered, for at least an hour, or till tender. (If you simmer it uncovered, you'll probably have to add more water since some will evaporate.) It is not necessary to add salt or anything, but it will be enhanced by flavoring the water with creole seasoning (basically salt, pepper, and red pepper), and quarters of an onion, a stalk of celery, and a carrot. These are usually discarded when the stock is strained (if not eaten!). When the meat is tender, remove it from the pot, allow it to cool enough to handle, then remove the meat from the bones and cut it into bite-size pieces. Remove any excessive oil from the top of the stock, then strain and save. It freezes beautifully should you have any left over. If you freeze it in ice cube trays, you have an excellent little cube of flavor to add to all kinds of soups, sauces, chowders, etc. If you have a slow cooker, the stock can be made overnight or while you are at work. I usually make my stock the day before I make gumbo; I prefer to remove the fat, and this is easy to do after it has hardened from refrigerating or freezing.

Shrimp stock can be made by peeling raw shrimp and

boiling the heads and peels (or just the peels) in seasoned water for about 20–30 minutes. Drain, discard the peels, and save that delicious stock! Boil fish heads for fish stock. A slow cooker works fine for this, too.

If using frozen, peeled shrimp, dried shrimp, or canned meat or seafood, then use canned chicken bouillon or broth. Or use bouillon cubes, granules, or soup base mixed with hot water (1 cube or teaspoon to 1 cup water). These usually have salt in them, so you may want to reduce the amount of salt in the recipe. Bottled clam juice subs well for seafood stock, and in my opinion is a nice enhancement to gumbos made with poultry or game.

Never throw any liquids away—they all add to the stock's flavor. Use the liquid from oysters, canned chicken, shrimp, clams, or crab meat, and canned tomatoes, and canned okra.

SEASONING:
½ teaspoon red pepper (Cayenne)
1 teaspoon salt
½ teaspoon thyme
2 bay leaves

Gumbo seasoning is very important. Most people like it mildly hot, but it's just a matter of preference. Crushed red pepper is excellent in place of the Cayenne or in addition to it; but be careful, it is very hot. Tabasco is quite good and has a flavor of its own. Two teaspoons would replace the ½ teaspoon Cayenne—or use them in combination, again at your own risk! A half of a fresh red pepper, chopped, is wonderful, but some peppers are hotter than others, so start out with just a total teaspoon and go from there. Black and white peppers are also excellent in combination with the red. Experiment lightly with pepper; you can always add more.

Other than red pepper, the most commonly used spices in gumbo are salt (or Lite Salt), thyme, and bay leaves. Use thyme alone or just ground or crushed bay leaves. If you use whole bay leaves, don't forget to take them out of the pot before serving. Other seasonings to try are oregano, nutmeg, allspice, cloves, chili powder, wine, lemon, vinegar, and probably anything you are brave enough to sprinkle or pour in. *K's Cajun Seasoning* is a delightful blend of spices that is so convenient, I cannot imagine having to measure out its many ingredients that are so often called for in Creole recipes. I heartily recommend you make a batch of it (see Contents); once you've used it, you'll never want to be without it.

MAIN INGREDIENTS:
2 pounds peeled shrimp, or
2 pounds cubed cooked chicken

Everything up to now is pretty basic for whatever kind of gumbo you are going to make. But here's where the "meat" of the gumbo is decided. Fresh anything is going to be more flavorful, of course, and combinations are even more delicious! Shrimp and chicken are suggested in this recipe because they are the most commonly used for gumbo. But almost any meat, fowl or seafood can be used. This includes turkey, guinea, duck, squirrel, goose, crab, venison, oyster, fish, ham, pork, sausage, beef, veal, etc.

All fresh seafood is put into the gumbo raw (except picked crab meat and crawfish tails which have already been boiled) only about 10–15 minutes before the end of cooking time, crabs in the shell a bit longer. If you cook seafood too long, it will get hard and rubbery and lose its taste.

Fowl can be cooked ahead of time, or in the gumbo,

allowing an hour or so for it to cook. I recommend cooking raw chicken in the gumbo pot only if the pieces are big. Be careful not to put anything with small bones to cook in the gumbo—it's too hard to see through the okra and vegetables and murky gumbo to get the small bones out!

Beef, pork and sausage can be added to the gumbo pot raw; again, allow an hour or so for them to cook through.

Cooked meat or fowl gets added one half hour or so before the end of cooking time.

RICE:
½–⅔ cup cooked rice per bowl

Use white rice prepared according to the package directions. If you plan to serve 5–6 bowls, cook one cup of raw rice (the yield is about 3½ cups cooked rice). Some recipes put the raw rice right in the pot, but most often gumbo is served over a scoop of steaming white, fluffy rice right in the bowl.

FINISHING TOUCHES:
Filé

Parsley

Green onions, chopped

There are those who put the filé powder into the gumbo along with the other seasonings. This is perfectly fine if you do not allow the gumbo to boil, and if it is to be served right away and there will probably be no leftovers. Ground sassafras leaves (filé) act as a thickening agent and have a pungent taste that is so uniquely associated with gumbo. But because its thickening power breaks down with boiling and reheating, and because it tends to become slightly bitter, it is best to either add the filé to the pot moments before serving, or simply offer it at the table to sprinkle over the rice or gumbo.

Parsley can be added anywhere along the cooking route. It can be added to the roux, with the tomatoes, to the stock, with the filé, or at the table! If you use dried parsley, add it to the pot; if you use freshly snipped, use it any time!

And lastly, chopped green onions are often added raw atop the steaming rice before pouring the gumbo into the bowls—a nice variation for onion lovers.

ACCOMPANIMENTS:

Hot, buttered French bread and a green salad are the traditional accompaniments to gumbo. Any salad— fruit, Jello, pasta, coleslaw—goes well with gumbo. Mamaw McKee always served potato salad and crackers with hers. Oyster crackers are nice to offer and toast points add a bit of elegance to a cup of gumbo before a meal. Sometimes baked potatoes (white or sweet) are served as a side dish. Since gumbo is not a heavy meal, dessert can be as fancy as you like, from light to lavish.

LAGNIAPPE:

Now here are a few extra pointers. All gumbos can be frozen. You may want to use a little less liquid to enable you to freeze it in smaller containers; add liquid when you reheat it. Do remove oysters before freezing—you can add fresh ones when you reheat.

And this bears repeating: make gumbo ahead of time so that all those marvelous flavors will have time to blend after the heat is turned off. Making and refrigerating it the day before your dinner party enables *you* to be fresh for your guests—the gumbo prefers a little aging.

And finally, you will notice that all the other recipes in this book vary in procedure, ingredients, and cooking methods. But now that you know the basics, any of these gumbos can be made for your next dinner party, family meal, or just for yourself. *Voila!*

A horse-drawn carriage in the New Orleans French Quarter.

MAMAW'S SHRIMP GUMBO
A family favorite . . . everybody loves it!

1 stick butter or margarine
1 pound frozen cut okra
⅔ cup vegetable oil
¾ cup flour
1 (12-ounce) bag frozen chopped onion
½ (10-ounce) bag frozen chopped bell pepper
3 quarts water
1 (28-ounce) can tomatoes, chopped
1 teaspoon chopped garlic
2 teaspoons salt
½ teaspoon ground bay leaves
½ teaspoon black pepper
1 teaspoon Tabasco
¼ teaspoon crushed red pepper
3–4 pounds raw shrimp, peeled

In big, heavy pot, melt butter; add okra and cook on medium heat till not ropy anymore—about 15–20 minutes—stirring often. In another big iron pot or skillet, heat and stir oil and flour to make dark brown roux. Add vegetables which have thawed slightly (the frozen kind sizzle a bit more, but keep stirring, it works just fine). Add a cup of hot water slowly to the roux, stirring till smooth. Now combine the two mixtures in the bigger pot.

Add tomatoes, water, garlic and all seasonings and bring to a boil. Add shrimp, bring back to a slight boil, lower heat and simmer about 30 minutes. Serve over fluffy rice with potato salad and buttered crackers and iced tea. Makes about 12–15 bowls.

NOTE: This was my mother-in-law's favorite gumbo; I often watched her make it and lovingly serve it to family and friends. She chopped fresh vegetables, of course, often from her own garden, which I heartily recommend. To save on time (and tears), I use the frozen, already-chopped vegetables in this gumbo without sacrificing its family-favorite flavor. I know Carrie McKee (from Folsom, Louisiana) would be pleased and proud to know her recipe was being shared by those who will be sure to serve her delicious gumbo as she did . . . with a lot of love.

THE MARINER'S GUMBO
A seafood gumbo culinary masterpiece!

5 strips bacon, diced
1 cup chopped onion
½ cup chopped green pepper
½ cup chopped celery
1 teaspoon minced garlic
1 teaspoon each: thyme, oregano, basil, black pepper,
chili powder, Tabasco
2½ quarts water
1 (28-ounce) can tomatoes, chopped
1 pound cut okra
1 pound diced fresh fish fillets,
(catfish, flounder, redfish)
2 pounds raw, peeled shrimp
½ pound cooked, diced scallops
½ pound fresh picked crab meat (optional)
½–1 cup white wine

Cook bacon in large, heavy pot and remove. Add vegetables and sauté till tender. Add spices, liquids, tomatoes and okra and cook 30 minutes. Add seafood and wine and cook another 30 minutes. Serve over hot rice. Serves 10–14 bowls.

NOTE: Gumbo is a hearty main course with a salad and French bread, but it is also most elegant served in a cup before dinner with little or no rice. Your guests will be so astounded at this elegant first course—the entrée will have a tough act to follow!

CATFISH GUMBO
This is incredibly delicious—try it!

3 pounds catfish, whole (or 2 pounds fillets)
6 cups water
1½ teaspoons salt
1 stick butter
3 tablespoons flour
1 cup chopped onion
1 cup chopped bell pepper
2 cups chopped celery
1 pound chopped okra
1 (28-ounce) can tomatoes, chopped
½ teaspoon *K's Cajun Seasoning* (or salt, pepper, and red pepper)
½ teaspoon thyme
1 tablespoon chopped parsley

Cook cleaned fish in boiling, salted water till it breaks apart with a fork (only takes a few minutes). Remove fish, debone, cut in chunks, and reserve stock. Melt butter in skillet; add flour and stir till lightly browned. Toss chopped vegetables into roux and heat till softened, stirring often. Mix everything together—except fish—in a pot with stock and simmer about an hour. Add fish and simmer 30–45 minutes. Serve over rice with a sprinkle of chopped parsley. Serves 8. Easy to make, incredibly delicious!

NOTE: Leftover cooked fish (be sure it passes the nose test!) is fine to add to *other* gumbos, but for this gumbo, you must use only fresh or freshly frozen mild fish in order to get that flavorful stock. Dried chopped onions can be substituted for real ones; mix ½ cup dried onions with ¾ cup very hot water, stir, and let sit. They fluff up nicely in about 10 minutes.

SNITCHER'S SEAFOOD GUMBO
Outstanding is an understatement!

½ cup olive oil
6 tablespoons flour
1½ cups chopped onions
½ cup chopped celery
½ cup chopped green pepper
2 teaspoons minced garlic
1 (10-ounce) package frozen cut okra
1 (1-pound) can tomatoes, chopped
2½ quarts water
1 teaspoon ground bay leaves
2 teaspoons Tabasco
1 tablespoon *K's Cajun Seasoning*,
(or salt and pepper)
½ teaspoon thyme
2 tablespoons chopped parsley
2–3 pounds raw shrimp, peeled
1 pound crab meat
2 pints oysters with liquid

Brown flour in olive oil in large heavy pot to make roux. Soften onions, celery and green pepper in roux. Add garlic, okra, tomatoes, and water, stirring to blend. Add remaining ingredients except seafood (but including oyster liquid) and bring to a boil. Lower heat and simmer 1 hour. Add shrimp, crab meat and oysters and cook about 15–20 minutes. Serve over fluffy rice. Makes 10–14 bowls.

NOTE: If you have "shrimp snitchers" and end up with too few shrimp in the second half of the pot, add more and cook another 10–15 minutes before serving.

AUNT TIEL'S FRESH CRAB
AND SHRIMP GUMBO
The best ever!

2–3 pounds fresh shrimp
½ fresh lemon, sliced
2¾ quarts water
5 strips bacon
¾ cup flour
4 stalks crisp celery, chopped
3 large onions, chopped
¼ pound butter
1 pound fresh okra, cut
3 large, fresh tomatoes, chopped
3 bay leaves
½ red pepper pod, cut
1 tablespoon salt
1 teaspoon freshly ground pepper
6 live crabs, plus 12 ounces picked crab meat

Clean and peel shrimp. Put heads and peels into large pot; refrigerate shrimp. Boil heads and peels with lemon slices in 2½ quarts water for about 30 minutes. When cool enough, strain and reserve broth.

Meanwhile fry bacon crisp and remove from pan. (Eat bacon to keep up your strength!) Brown flour in bacon fat on medium heat, stirring till brown. Add onions and celery; stir till vegetables are limp. Stir in a cup of hot water and transfer to very large pot. Melt butter in skillet and cook okra slowly till not too stringy. Stir in tomatoes till mixed. Transfer to big pot with shrimp stock in it. Add seasonings. Let this come to a boil, then simmer forever (about 3 hours!). Now add live crabs and boil gently about 20 minutes. Add picked crab meat and shrimp and cook another 15–20 minutes till shrimp are pink. Remove bay leaves. Serve over rice. Makes 8–10 servings.

NOTE: When my great Aunt Tiel made gumbo, it was

an event. She actually bought 12 crabs which she insisted on choosing herself. She called the market to see when they were coming in so she was assured of getting them *fresh*. (Short of fishing them out of the water herself and personally coaxing selected beauties to follow her home and jump into her gumbo pot, these crabs were as fresh as she could get them!) They had to be the right color and size and lively! The bringing in of the crabs was quite exciting to us children and there were many squeals and laughs when they were "poured" into the sink for their bath before going you-know-where! After boiling, she cooled them enough to pick, adeptly getting that wonderfully choice meat out of those thin shells. She saved six bodies (with the shell, legs, "dead man's fingers," and underside "sand bag" removed) which she broke in half, and six sets of claws to put into the gumbo pot whole.

Making gumbo was a whole-day affair that we enjoyed preparing (watching) as much as eating when we visited Aunt Tiel in New Orleans or when she visited us in Baton Rouge. Her gumbo was unquestionably *fresh*, and every time she made it, we all agreed, it was her best ever!

24-KARAT GUMBO
Rich . . . *in every sense of the word!*

2 pounds raw shrimp in shells
3 quarts water
3 lemon slices
3 bay leaves
1 teaspoon *K's Cajun Seasoning*
(or salt and pepper)
½ cup vegetable oil
⅔ cup flour
2 cups chopped onions
1 cup chopped celery
½ cup chopped bell pepper
1 (16-ounce) can tomatoes, chopped
3 (10-ounce) packages frozen cut okra
2 teaspoons minced garlic
2 tablespoons each: chopped parsley, Tabasco,
Worcestershire
1½ teaspoons each: salt, black pepper, dried basil
2 cups cooked chicken, torn to bite size
4 crabs with claws, cleaned and quartered (or 12 ounces
picked crab meat)
12–16 oysters with liquid
Filé
Chopped green onions

Boil shrimp in water with lemon, bay leaves and "K's." Boil 1 minute, then remove shrimp to platter to cool. Discard lemon and bay leaves; reserve stock. Make roux by browning flour and oil. Add roux to stock pot along with remaining ingredients except seafood, filé, and green onions; simmer 30 minutes.

Peel shrimp and add to stock with other seafood. Cook gently about 20–30 minutes. Serve over rice and pass the filé and green onions. Serves 12–15 impressively.

NOTE: This 24-ingredient gumbo is truly a magnificant feast! A little more trouble, a little more expense. . . . Go for it! It's worth it!

CREOLE ROUX SEAFOOD GUMBO
So thick you can almost eat it with a fork!

3 tablespoons vegetable oil
1 pound cut okra
1 recipe *Creole Roux* (see Contents)
3–4 pounds shrimp, peeled
1 pound crab meat
3 quarts water
½ cup green onions
3 tablespoons chopped parsley
Steamed rice

In heavy stock pot, heat oil and stir in cut okra. Cook slowly, stirring often to keep from sticking. When okra is no longer ropy, add *Creole Roux* and cook 20–30 minutes. Add shrimp, crab meat, and water. Simmer about 20–30 minutes. Add chopped onion tops and parsley 15 minutes before serving. Serve over hot rice. Makes 10–12 servings.

NOTE: Shrimp must not be added till near the end of cooking time—overcooking toughens them. However, in that short cooking time, the flavor of the shrimp will not fully blend into the gumbo. That is why gumbo is more flavorful the day after you make it or after freezing—at the very least, try to serve several hours after you make it. If you do not have to serve right away, turn the heat off, let it cool slightly, then refrigerate the gumbo right in its cooking pot. Reheat all or part of it while cooking the rice. It's easy to reheat individual bowls in the microwave, but do be careful not to overheat it— meat and seafood toughen very quickly.

CUP O' CRAB GUMBO
Easy enough for a beginner—exquisite enough for a queen!

1 cup chopped green onions
1 cup chopped celery
1 stick real butter
3 tablespoons flour
1 cup finely cut okra (optional)
1 (1-pound) can cream style corn
3 cloves garlic, minced
¼ teaspoon nutmeg
1 teaspoon honey (or sugar)
1½ teaspoons salt
½ teaspoon white pepper
1 quart water
1 pound fresh lump crab meat
Fresh snipped parsley

In Dutch oven, sauté onions and celery in butter till soft. Mix in flour and stir till barely brown. Stir in okra, cooking till soft, about 10 minutes. Add remaining ingredients except crab meat and parsley. Bring to a boil, lower heat, cover and simmer 10 minutes. Add crab meat which has been picked for shells; stir and cook another 15 minutes, then turn heat off. Serve over hot rice, if desired, with a sprinkle of snipped parsley. Superb on its own with toast points or dainty crackers. Serves 6–10.

NOTE: This elegant gumbo can be prepared in about a half hour and served right away. You won't think it possible, but it is even more delectable after it has had a day of rest in the refrigerator (or a fortnight in the freezer!). It is so simple and so simply good! Curry powder or mace can be substituted for the nutmeg for equally delicious variations. Fun to serve in crockery custard cups, but definitely deserving of your best bone china. Be sure to use real butter for maximum flavor. You may have to add a bit more water if serving over rice as this is creamy and thick . . . and delightfully delicate.

SPICY HOT CROCK POT GUMBO
Perfect before dinner cup o' gumbo;
the rice is cooked in!

1 recipe *Microwave Roux*
4 ounces cooked cubed ham
1 (14½-ounce) can cut okra
½ (10-ounce) can Rotel tomatoes, chopped
3 cups hot water
¼ teaspoon allspice (optional)
1 tablespoon brown sugar
½ cup converted rice
½ teaspoon ground bay leaves
½ teaspoon Creole Crab Boil (optional)
½ teaspoon salt
2 pounds raw peeled shrimp
1 tablespoon filé

Put all but shrimp in crock pot and stir well. Cover and cook on HIGH 2–3 hours or till rice is tender. Add shrimp and cook on HIGH 15–25 minutes till shrimp are cooked through. Add filé to pot or sprinkled on gumbo bowls or cups. Serve immediately with oyster crackers.

NOTE: The Rotel tomatoes are quite spicy, so don't add any extra pepper. Use the whole can if you like it hot. This makes about 8–10 bowls or 20–24 cups. It can be cooked conventionally on top of the stove in one hour, but you'll have to add more water—slow cookers retain more of their liquids. Or cook it on the low setting of your slow cooker 5–8 hours, depending on how slow your cooker is (or how long you want to leave it)!

HOT CRAWFISH GUMBO
A springtime treat!

¾ cup vegetable oil
¾ cup flour
1 cup onions, chopped
1 cup celery, chopped
½ cup chopped bell pepper
½ cup chopped green onions
1 (8-ounce) can tomato sauce
½–1 (10-ounce) can Rotel tomatoes
1 (14½-ounce) can chicken broth
2 quarts water
2 tablespoons fresh snipped parsley
1 teaspoon minced garlic
1½ teaspoons salt
1 teaspoon Creole Crab Boil (optional)
2–3 pounds peeled crawfish tails
Filé

Make dark roux of flour and oil. Stir in onions, celery, bell pepper and green onions till soft. Stir in tomato sauce, then tomatoes, broth, and water. Simmer 1–1½ hours. Add remaining ingredients except filé and simmer 20–30 minutes. Serve on rice with filé. Serves 10–12.

NOTE: A crawfish boil is a fun outdoor springtime party, usually in April or May when the crawfish are running (in season). When everyone has consumed all they can eat, the remaining crawfish tails are peeled while the party is still going on . . . ready for étouffée or bisque . . . or the gumbo pot the next day!

Cypress trees and knees in Louisiana's swampland.

SEAFOOD OVEN OKRA GUMBO
For those who like to plan ahead

OVEN OKRA:
3 pounds okra, sliced
3 onions, chopped
3 ribs celery, chopped
3 cloves garlic, minced
1 (28-ounce) can tomatoes, chopped
1 (6-ounce) can tomato paste
1 teaspoon *K's Cajun Seasoning,*
(or salt and pepper)

Combine all in large heavy pot. Cover and cook 2 hours in 300-degree oven, stirring twice during cooking. Uncover and cook another 20 minutes. Makes enough for 2 pots of gumbo. This can be halved or doubled; freeze portions for later quick-fixin gumbo!

3–4 cups *Oven Okra*
2 quarts water
½ cup *Dry Roux* (see Contents)
2 pounds peeled uncooked shrimp
8–10 crabs, cleaned, halved or 1 (6-ounce) can crab
meat
1½ teaspoons *K's Cajun Seasoning* (or salt and pepper)

Mix roux in ½ cup cold water. Stir into *Oven Okra.* Add remaining water. Bring to a boil, then add seafood; season. Cook 30 minutes. Serve over hot rice. Serves 8–10.

NOTE: Add chicken stock and most any poultry, seafood, or meat to *Oven Okra* to create your own special gumbo concoction quick!

TURKEY OVEN OKRA GUMBO

1 turkey leg and thigh,
(or equivalent meat from carcass)
2½ quarts water
2½ teaspoons *K's Cajun Seasoning,*
(or salt, pepper and red pepper)
¾ cup *Dry Roux* (optional)
3–4 cups *Oven Okra* (see opposite page)
1½ teaspoons crab boil (optional)

Boil turkey in large pot with 1½ teaspoons seasoning while *Oven Okra* is cooking. Remove turkey when tender, cool slightly, then debone and cut in chunks; reserve stock. Dissolve *Dry Roux* in ¾ cup cold water, stirring till smooth. Add to *Oven Okra* and stir well. Add okra to turkey stock, then add turkey and seasonings. Heat thoroughly. Serves 8–10.

NOTE: Crab boil is available in many parts of the country in liquid in a small bottle, granulated in a round shaker box, or in a square box containing bags of whole seasonings for dropping in the boiling pot of seafood. Use whichever you can find, but don't open the seasoning bags—drop one in briefly and remove.

CHICKEN 'N' SAUSAGE FILÉ GUMBO
No okra! No tomatoes! Pass the filé, please.

3 pounds chicken thighs
K's Cajun Seasoning,
(or salt and pepper)
½ cup vegetable oil
1 cup flour
1 cup minced onion
½ cup minced bell pepper
½ cup minced celery
1 teaspoon Tabasco sauce
3 tablespoons Worcestershire
½ teaspoon ground bay leaves
1 teaspoon *K's Cajun Seasoning,*
(or salt and pepper)
2¼ quarts hot water
½ cup sliced green onions
3 cloves minced garlic
1 pound smoked pork sausage, thinly sliced
Filé

Remove skin from chicken thighs, clean and pat dry with paper towels. Season all over with K's. Heat oil in large, heavy pot. Sear chicken; remove and set aside. Make roux by adding flour to hot oil in pot. Stir constantly over medium high heat till medium brown. Stir onion, bell pepper, and celery into roux; cook until tender. Return chicken to pot and add Tabasco, Worcestershire, bay leaves and K's. Cover and allow to simmer one hour. Add green onions, garlic and sausage. Stir, cover and simmer another hour. Remove all thigh bones from gumbo. Skim off excess oil (or refrigerate and easily remove hardened fat before reheating). Serve in bowls over hot rice and pass the filé. Serves 10–14 bowls.

NOTE: This is a wonderfully hearty and robust gumbo made especially for those who think they don't like okra.

Though other chicken parts may be used, the thigh bones are the easiest to remove. Serve with a tossed green salad, lots of garlic-buttered French bread, and a big pitcher of lemony iced tea. Delicious!

CHICKEN CROCK POT GUMBO
Put it on and let it do its thing!

1 recipe *Microwave Roux*
2 strips bacon, cubed
3 cups boneless, skinless chicken, cut to bite size
1 (10-ounce) package frozen cut okra
5 cups hot water
4 chicken bouillon cubes
1 tablespoon brown sugar
1 teaspoon *K's Cajun Seasoning,*
(or salt and pepper)
1 (8-ounce) can tomato sauce (optional)
2 teaspoons parsley flakes (optional)
1 (6-ounce) can clams or shrimp (optional)
Filé

Fry bacon pieces lightly, not crisp. Pour bacon and all ingredients except seafood into crock pot and stir well. Cook on low all night or all day (8 hours or so). Add seafood 10 minutes before turning pot off; stir, cover, and let sit while you cook the rice. Serve over rice with filé. Serves 8–10.

NOTE: Crock pot cooking retains liquid, so even with okra and roux, it likes a little filé, too.

GOMBO FILÉ AUX POULET
(Chicken Filé Gumbo)

2–3 pounds meaty chicken pieces
1 ham hock
2 cups cut okra
2 onions, chopped
2 tomatoes, chopped
Salt, pepper, red pepper, garlic powder to taste
7–8 cups water
3 tablespoons flour
3 tablespoons bacon fat
2 teaspoons filé
2 dozen oysters
Tabasco

Put chicken, ham hock, okra, onion, tomatoes, and seasoning in water in big iron pot. Cook till meat is tender. Debone chicken and cut meat into small pieces. Make roux of flour and fat in iron skillet and add to pot. Cook 15 minutes. Stir in filé and oysters and cook till edges curl. Serve over scoops of rice. Makes 8–12 bowls.

NOTE: This is a well-used recipe from a friend who got it from a salty old Cajun who insisted you had to have a black iron pot, that ingredients had to be estimated, and whose total instructions were: "Cook it tillis done, den odd dem oyster an sassafras leave, maybe tree/two shakes hot sauce in dah bowl." They say he sat down to his gumbo with his filé and Tabasco at his side and actually did his deboning and devouring at the same time. He cooked a simple, stout gumbo, and knew that filé (ground sassafras leaves) should be added just before serving, as boiling will break down its thickening power and reheating may impair the flavor. His gumbo was *très bon.* I couldn't agree more.

Swamp Gardens in the southern Atchafalaya. Morgan City.

HENNY-PENNY FILÉ GUMBO
The filé is cooked in the gumbo

1 fat hen
2½ quarts water
1 teaspoon *K's Cajun Seasoning,*
(or salt and pepper)
½ cup oil
¾ cup flour
1 (8-ounce) bottle clam juice
2 onions, chopped
2 stalks celery, chopped
1 (10-ounce) package frozen cut okra
1 (1-pound) can stewed tomatoes
½ teaspoon each: salt, black pepper, chili powder,
thyme, garlic powder
1 tablespoon paprika
1 teaspoon brown sugar
2 tablespoons snipped parsley
2 tablespoons filé
Chopped green onion, if desired

Boil hen in seasoned water to cover. Remove and debone when tender, saving broth. Make roux of flour and oil, stirring constantly in black iron skillet till chocolate brown. Transfer to stock pot and add clam juice. Add vegetables and seasonings except parsley and filé. Heat thoroughly, then cook on low heat 1½ hours; add torn-into-bite size hen pieces, parsley and filé. Cook 15–30 minutes. Serve on mounds of rice with a sprinkle of chopped green onion. Serves 8–12.

NOTE: If you plan to freeze a portion of this gumbo, do not cook the filé in it, but add it to the serving bowls. Easy to crock pot henny-penny all night before making gumbo the following day.

LEAN AND MEAN CHICKEN GUMBO
Anything this good must be fattening
Right? . . . WRONG!

2–3 pounds chicken breasts
K's Cajun Seasoning (made with Lite Salt),
(or Lite Salt and pepper)
2 tablespoons flour
3 tablespoons low fat margarine, divided
2 cups cut okra
1 cup tomatoes, chopped
1 cup chopped onions
3 tablespoons *Oven-baked Dry Roux*
3 quarts water
½ teaspoon red pepper
Lite Salt and pepper to taste
Steamed rice

Skin and wash chicken breasts. Dredge chicken in seasoned flour. In large, heavy pot, sear chicken in 1½ tablespoons margarine. Remove chicken to plate. Fry okra and onion in remaining 1½ tablespoons margarine, then stir in tomatoes and roux. Debone chicken, cut in bite-size pieces, and return to pot. Add water and seasonings. Bring to a slight boil, then simmer, covered, at least an hour. Serve over ½ cup hot rice. Offer filé. Makes 8–12 bowls.

NOTE: Use either fresh or frozen okra, and either fresh or canned tomatoes. This is sooooo good. Try it even if you're not calorie conscious. Yum!

MICROWAVE CHICKEN 'N' SAUSAGE GUMBO

1 recipe *Microwave Roux*
1 (10-ounce) package frozen cut okra
3 cups chicken broth, heated
1 (8-ounce) bottle clam juice (optional)
2 cups hot water
1 (10-ounce) can Rotel tomatoes, chopped
2 teaspoons *K's Cajun Seasoning,*
(or salt and pepper)
½ teaspoon ground bay leaves
3 cups cooked chicken (or turkey), bite size
½ pound smoked sausage, diced
Filé

Place unwrapped carton of okra on a plate and microwave on HIGH 7 minutes. In a 5-quart casserole, mix together roux, okra, broth, juice, hot water, tomatoes and seasonings. Cover and cook on HIGH 12 minutes. Add chicken and sausage. Cover and cook on HIGH another 12 minutes. Skim oil from top. Serve over fluffy rice with a sprinkle of filé.

NOTE: Though this is quite flavorful and certainly quicker to fix than stove-top gumbos, the vegetables do not cook to pieces quite as much and it makes a thinner broth. You may want to add ⅓ cup *Dry Roux* mixed with ⅓ cup cold water along with the meat before the final cooking. This is delicious right now, but tomorrow it'll be even better!

THE TAIL OF THE TURKEY GUMBO
This story has a very happy ending.

Turkey bones (with 1–2 pounds meat left on)
Water to cover
2 teaspoons *K's Cajun Seasoning,*
(or salt and pepper)
¾ cup flour
¾ cup oil or bacon drippings
2 onions, chopped
1 bell pepper, chopped
3 stalks celery, chopped
1½ teaspoons minced garlic
2 quarts turkey stock
1 (1-pound) can tomatoes, chopped
½ teaspoon ground bay leaves
½ teaspoon dried basil
¼ teaspoon red pepper (optional)
1 pound ham, diced

Place turkey carcass in stock pot with water to cover, sprinkle "K's" on top, stir and let boil about 1½ hours. Remove carcass and meat; reserve broth. Cut turkey into bite-size pieces. Brown flour in oil to make a dark roux. Add vegetables and stir till soft. Stir in a cup or so of hot stock, then pour roux into stock pot with reserved broth. Cook ½ hour, then add tomatoes, turkey, seasonings, and ham and cook another ½ hour. Serve with rice. Offer filé and Tabasco. Serves 8–10.

NOTE: This is such a perfect thing to do with the carcass of the Thanksgiving turkey . . . so good it's often looked forward to as much as the Thanksgiving meal itself! Is this an Easter turkey? Then you may want to put some peeled Easter eggs (leave whole) in the gumbo pot right before serving, one for each bowl . . . Violà! *Easter Bunny Gumbo!*

DUCK 'N' ANDOUILLE GUMBO
Most any wild game can sit in for the duck!

3–4 cleaned and washed ducks
Water, salt and pepper
1 large (2 small) onions, quartered
2 stalks celery
3 bay leaves
1 teaspoon garlic salt

Boil ducks in large pot with seasoned water to cover. Add remaining ingredients. Bring to a boil and simmer 1 hour until tender. Remove ducks, cool slightly, then debone. Chill stock. Remove hardened fat from top.

¾ cup flour
¾ cup oil (bacon fat, if desired)
1½ cups chopped onions
½ cup chopped celery
½ cup chopped bell pepper
2 teaspoons minced garlic
2 thinly sliced carrots
2 tablespoons snipped parsley
3 quarts stock
¼ cup port red wine
2 teaspoons salt
¼ teaspoon red pepper
½ teaspoon black pepper
2 bay leaves
Duck meat, cut bite size
1 pound Andouille (smoked sausage), diced
18–24 oysters, cut, if big (optional)
⅓ cup finely chopped green onion tops
Filé

Make dark brown roux with oil and flour in big, heavy pot. Add vegetables and cook till tender. Stir in stock (add water and a chicken bouillon cube if you do not have enough to make 3 quarts), wine and seasonings. Now add duck and sausage, bring to a boil and simmer 1 hour. Add oysters, cook 15–20 minutes, till oysters curl. Remove bay leaves. Serve over rice, with green onions and filé offered at the table.

NOTE: As a general rule, game is a little tougher, needs a little more cooking, a little more seasoning, and is enhanced by either using bacon fat for the roux and/or sausage or ham in the pot with it. Try smoking the ducks instead of boiling them for an extra exciting flavor.

I used to date a fellow whose family loved to hunt. Pappy made jambalayas and stews and gumbos from the rabbit, squirrel, dove, turkey, deer—whatever they brought home—that were always unbelievably delicious (even though I always had to ask what I was eating). The flavor of wild game cooked in the Creole fashion is absolutely outstanding and unequaled.

On Kent House Plantation. Alexandria.

BURGUNDY BEEF GUMBO
The full-bodied flavor is so hearty and good!

2 tablespoons vegetable oil
1½ pounds lean stew meat or round steak, cut in very
small cubes
½ pound ham, cubed
1 (20-ounce) bag frozen cut okra
2 teaspoons *K's Cajun Seasoning,*
(or salt, pepper and red pepper to taste)
3 quarts hot water
1 beef bouillon cube
½ teaspoon Kitchen Bouquet
½ cup Burgundy wine
2 tablespoons vegetable oil
2 tablespoons flour
2 onions, finely chopped
½ bell pepper, finely chopped
1 teaspoon minced garlic

Brown meat lightly in oil in large, heavy pot. Add ham and stir. Cook about 5 minutes. Remove meat and cook okra in drippings, stirring occasionally till it loses its ropyness. Return meat to pot and season. Stir in 1 cup of boiling water in which 1 beef bouillon cube has been dissolved. Now add Kitchen Bouquet, wine and remaining water and bring to a boil. Lower heat, cover and simmer for 1 hour.

Now make roux with flour and oil, stirring in heavy skillet over medium heat till nicely brown. Add chopped onions, bell pepper, and garlic and stir till soft. Stir in 1 cup hot water, then add roux to meat pot. Simmer covered another hour. Serve over rice with filé offered. Serves 8–10.

NOTE: Kitchen Bouquet adds a dark brown color as well as adding flavor. Bouillon adds flavor, but it also adds salt, so taste before you salt further. Taste the wine, too (you want to be sure it's the right heartiness for this robust gumbo!)

PORK ROAST GUMBO
Absolutely outstanding!

1 (3-pound) pork shoulder picnic or Boston butt roast
3½ quarts water
1 tablespoon dried onion flakes
2 teaspoons *K's Cajun Seasoning* (or salt and pepper)
3 tablespoons bacon drippings
4 tablespoons flour
1½ cups chopped onions
½ stick butter or margarine
3 cups cut okra
1 teaspoon minced garlic
1 teaspoon Tabasco
1 teaspoon brown sugar
2 bay leaves
½ pound diced ham, optional
Filé

Boil inexpensive cut of pork roast in water seasoned with onion flakes and 1 teaspoon of the *K's Cajun Seasoning* (or salt and pepper) till tender (about 1½ hours). Remove meat to chopping board and when cool enough to handle, cut meat from bone in very small pieces. Put meat back in the stock.

Make roux in iron pot with bacon drippings and flour, stirring over medium heat till cocoa brown. Stir in chopped onions; cook 3 minutes; add to stock pot.

In same roux skillet, cook okra in melted butter about 10 minutes. Add okra and all remaining ingredients to stock and cook another hour. Remove bay leaves. Serve over rice with filé. Serves 12–15.

NOTE: This gumbo is very inexpensive to make and smells so good cooking, they'll all come running (including the dog, who will gladly help dispose of the bone).

Most Cajuns wouldn't dream of making a roux in anything but an iron skillet. Besides being ideal for evenly browning the flour, it is actually healthier. It is a fact that some of the iron from the skillet is released in the food and passed on to the consumer. No kidding! Could be why there are so many lively old Cajuns!

MOULIN-ROUGE GUMBO
If you can open a can . . .

½ stick butter or margarine
2 tablespoons flour
1 (1-pound) can okra
1 (11-ounce) can chicken broth
1 (12-ounce) can tomato juice
2 juice cans of water
1 (5-ounce) can boned chicken
½ teaspoon *K's Cajun Seasoning* (or salt, pepper, and red pepper)
3 tablespoons dried chopped onions
½ teaspoon garlic (granulated, powdered or fresh minced)
3 (6-ounce) cans seafood (shrimp, clams, crab meat, any combination)
1 teaspoon filé

In Dutch oven, brown butter and flour lightly on medium heat. Stir in remaining ingredients except seafood and filé. Bring to a boil, lower heat and simmer 20–30 minutes. Add seafood with all juices and filé; stir and simmer another 10 minutes. Remove from heat, cover and let sit another 30 minutes. Serve over rice (boil-in-a-bag is easiest) in bowls. Serves 4–6.

NOTE: Serve with a canned drink. (Just kidding!)

CROWD PLEASING GUMBO
This will feed 50—you'll need a big pot!

3 cups flour
3 cups oil
5 pounds onions, chopped
1 bunch celery, finely chopped
4 bell peppers, finely chopped
1 pound butter or margarine
6 pounds cut okra
1 (28-ounce) can tomatoes, chopped
1 (10-ounce) can Rotel tomatoes, chopped
1 (6-ounce) can tomato paste
3 gallons water
¼ cup Worcestershire
¼ cup *K's Cajun Seasoning* (or salt and pepper)
1 tablespoon each: thyme, basil, ground bay leaves,
garlic powder, Tabasco
Red pepper to taste
8–10 pounds fresh shrimp, peeled
4 pounds fresh catfish fillets, bite size
½ cup snipped parsley

Brown flour in oil in big iron Dutch oven pot or skillet. Add vegetables and stir till soft. Stir in 2 cups hot water slowly. In a *big* stock pot (or use 2 pots and divide everything), melt butter and add cut okra. Cook over medium heat, stirring occasionally till okra loses its ropyness. Add chopped tomatoes, tomato paste, roux, water, and all seasonings. Let come to a boil, lower heat and simmer 1 hour, covered. Add shrimp, fish, and parsley. Serve over hot rice. Have filé on hand.

NOTE: Do this the day before your party, *please*. And get a friend to help—makes it more fun and it goes a lot quicker. If you need to cut back on the expense, substitute 4–5 chickens cooked in their stock for the seafood. And you may throw in a pound or two of cut-up smoked sausage or 2 pints oysters, cut. Gumbo doesn't have to be expensive—the kind I cook is usually dictated by what is on hand or on sale at the market!

OKRA AND TOMATO GUMBO
Five 1-cup ingredients and a little seasoning

2 tablespoons bacon drippings or butter
1 cup chopped onions
1 cup chopped bell peppers
1 cup chopped tomatoes
1 cup sliced okra
1 cup hot water
¼ teaspoon oregano
½ teaspoon *K's Cajun Seasoning,*
(or sprinklings of salt, pepper, red pepper,
ground bay leaves and garlic powder)

Melt butter in heavy pot; stir in onions and peppers till soft. Add remaining ingredients. Cook over medium heat till thick, stirring often. Serves 4.

NOTE: This is simple and so thick it can almost be eaten with a fork! Try adding some sliced, fresh mushrooms. Serve with toast points. Add more water if you want to serve over rice. Serves 4.

Z'HERBES GUMBO
This marvelous greens gumbo was created by superstition

1 pound lean salt meat
4 quarts water
1 small head cabbage, shredded
1 teaspoon salt
2 (10-ounce) packages frozen chopped spinach
1 (10-ounce) package frozen chopped mustard greens
1 (10-ounce) package frozen chopped turnip greens
3 tablespoons flour
3 tablespoons vegetable oil
1½ cups chopped onions
1 cup chopped green onions
2 tablespoons fresh snipped parsley
2 teaspoons minced garlic
1 tablespoon sugar
½ teaspoon ground bay leaves
2 tablespoons vinegar
1 pod of red pepper or ¼ teaspoon red pepper
Salt and pepper to taste

Rinse salt meat, cut in chunks, and boil in 2½ quarts of water in a big stock pot till tender (about 1½ hours). Remove meat; chop lean portions of meat when cool; discard fat; reserve broth. Cook shredded cabbage in the broth about 15 minutes.

In another big pot, bring 1½ quarts of salted water to a boil. Place frozen spinach and greens in the boiling water and cook till done—about 20 minutes.

While greens are cooking, make a roux of flour and oil by stirring constantly in an iron skillet on medium high heat. When nicely brown, add chopped onions and green onions. Now put everything in the biggest pot, including parsley, meat, and seasonings. Cook another 20 minutes or so while you are making cornbread. Serve over rice, if desired. Serves 10–12. Freezes well.

NOTE: This is a truly delicious "gumbo vert" (green gumbo). The superstition in Cajun country (South Louisiana) was that if you ate seven greens on Holy Thursday and met seven people on Good Friday, you would have good luck all year, and that is how *Z'Herbes Gumbo* was born. A few insisted you must eat nine greens, so in addition to the ones above, it often included collard greens, watercress, radish tops, parsley, chicory, bell pepper, kale, green onions, beet tops and/or carrot tops. Fresh greens are wonderful, of course, and you can chop them before or after cooking. I added too much red pepper one time, so I threw in a quartered potato to soften the bite—it was delicious! And cornbread is a *must* with *Z'Herbes Gumbo!*

A misty morning view of St. Louis Cathedral. New Orleans.

ABOUT THE AUTHOR

Gwen McKee was born, raised, and educated (LSU) in Baton Rouge, and was exposed at an early age to the wonderful cuisine of South Louisiana. As director of her own publishing company, (Quail Ridge Press), Gwen personally edits all the cookbooks published by her company. She enjoys testing and refining the recipes included in the QRP cookbooks as well as traveling to promote and sell the books. Of particular pleasure was the opportunity to develop and publish *The Best of the Best from Louisiana* (QRP, 1984), a highly acclaimed cookbook that features favorite recipes from fifty of Louisiana's leading cookbooks. This project sharpened her already acute interest in Louisiana cooking and led to the development of a book that is entirely devoted to one of her very favorite dishes . . . gumbo.

Now making her home in Brandon, Mississippi, Gwen and husband, Barney (of 26 years), have a daughter, Heather, two sons, Brian and Shawn, and a daughter-in-law, Betsy.

Quail Ridge Press cookbooks contain superb, carefully selected and tested recipes that are fun to read, easy to follow, and guaranteed to bring rave results! These attractively produced books are a delight to discover, to give, to receive and to use. The $5.95 gift series includes: *The Twelve Days of Christmas Cookbook, The Seven Chocolate Sins, A Salad A Day, Quickies for Singles, The Country Mouse Cheese Cookbook,* and *Hors D'Oeuvres Everybody Loves.* The QRP Best of the Best Series includes: *Best of the Best from Texas* $14.95, *Best of the Best from Louisiana* $12.95, *Best of the Best from Mississippi* $12.95, *Best of the Best from Florida* $12.95, *Best of the Best from Tennessee* $12.95, *Best of the Best from Kentucky* $12.95, *Best of the Best from Alabama* $12.95, and *Best of the Best from Georgia* $14.95. Other cookbooks are *Gourmet Camping* $10.95 and *The Little Bean Book* $9.95.

The Little Gumbo Book is $6.95. Send $1.05 postage for first book ordered and 50¢ for each additional copy, along with check, money order or Visa/MC number and expiration date to:

QRP DISTRIBUTION CENTER
P.O. BOX 123
Brandon, MS 39043

To order by phone call toll free: 1/800/343-1583
Mississippi residents call collect 825-2063